Contents

Some words are shown in bold, **like this**.
You can find them in the glossary on page 23.

What kind of pet is this?

Pets are animals that live with us.

Some pets are small and furry.

My pet is small and has feathers.

Can you guess what kind of
pet it is?

What are birds?

Birds are animals that have feathers and lay eggs.

There are many kinds of pet bird.

Some birds come from warm places.

These birds are sometimes kept
as pets.

Where did my bird come from?

This mother bird laid a **clutch** of eggs in a **nest**.

Young birds hatched from the eggs.

The birds stayed in the nest for five or six weeks.

Then, we chose one from the pet shop to take home.

How big is my bird?

Some birds are very small when they hatch.

They are about the size of an adult's thumb.

When they grow up they are bigger.

Some are as long as an adult's foot.

Where does my bird live?

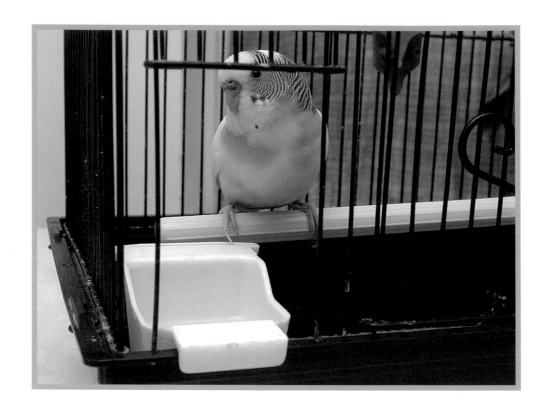

Pet birds need a big cage to live in.

My bird sits on a **perch** in its cage.

Some birds can come out of their cages.

My bird can sit on a special ladder.

What does my bird eat?

My bird eats bird seed.

Sometimes it eats fruit, too.

Many birds eat vegetables.

My bird sometimes eats lettuce.

What else does my bird need?

All birds need to drink water.

Sometimes my bird drinks a little juice or milk.

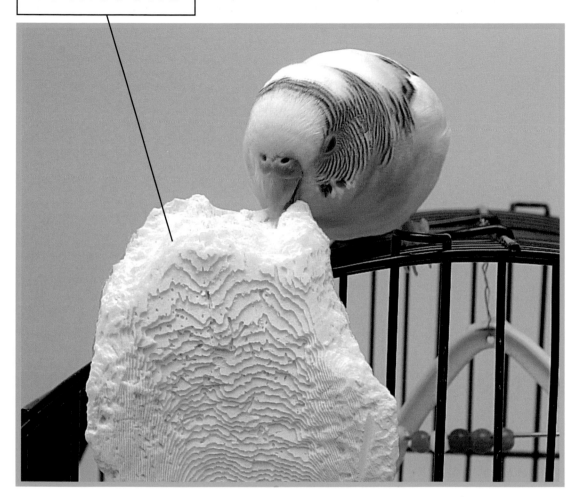

cuttlebone

Birds need **minerals**.

Cuttlebone is a bird treat with lots of minerals.

What can I do for my bird?

paper

I can keep the bird cage clean.

I change the paper and wash the food dishes every day.

I cover the bird cage at night.

This helps my bird to rest and stay warm.

What can my bird do?

My bird can play games.

It can play fetch with a toy ball.

My bird can do tricks, too.

It can ring a bell.

Bird map

eye

feathers

beak

tail

claws

Glossary

clutch
group of two or more eggs or baby birds

cuttlebone
healthy treat given to birds to eat

minerals
something the body needs so that it can work properly and stay healthy

nest
shelter made by a bird for its eggs and babies

perch
bar or branch a bird uses to rest on with its claws

Index